C000103691

Dedicated to:

YOU.

And your search for

TRUE LOVE.

WANT A SUPER COOL BOOK FROM US FOR ✨FREE?✨ (WHAAAAAAAT)?

(ALSO, WE WANT TO SEND YOU SOME EXTRA LOVE BECAUSE YOU DON'T HAVE A BOYFRIEND RIGHT NOW)

pictures, quotes & affirmations to create the ultimate vision board

print-ready

$8.99 value, free

with over 65 full color elements

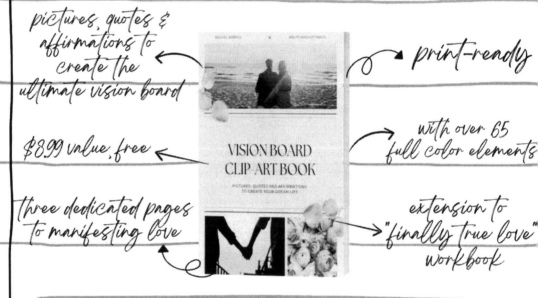

three dedicated pages to manifesting love

extension to "finally true love" workbook

EMAIL US AT:

wmp.freebook@gmail.com

with subject line: TRUELOVE

and we will send you your free copy!

YES, I WANNA!

COPYRIGHT, 2023 WRITE MINDSET PRESS

60 DAYS TO TRUE LOVE

PART 1: THE ONE IN WHICH
I UNVEIL THE MAN I DEEPLY DESIRE

PART 2: THE ONE IN WHICH
I KNOW MY WORTH AND BELIEVE IN IT

PART 3: THE ONE IN WHICH
I MANIFEST TRUE LOVE

Day 56	I am loved
Day 57	Manifesting my soulmate
Day 58	Alignment with the universe
Day 59	Grateful for my soulmate
Day 60	Making a real vision board

You deserve true love

You know that once-in-a-lifetime, dream-come-true kind of love your soul has been waiting for? The kind of love that will make every cup of coffee you've sipped sitting alone at a cafe, every lonely night you've spent in bed wondering if you'll ever be in a real, fulfilling relationship, and every date that made your cheeks hurt from faking a smile and head hurt from pointless conversations- SEEM ALL WORTH IT?

You are meant to experience that kind of love.

Even if you have an image in mind of a high quality man, but believe you don't deserve that man, because "why will he choose to be with me?", you are meant to experience that kind of love.

Even if you always seem to meet and date the wrong kind of people, and don't get a text back from the rare one you like, you are meant to experience that kind of love.

Even if you constantly bounce between hope and despair, between believing in miracles and disregarding them, between wishing each date to be "the one" and coming back home with an unexplained heaviness in your heart, you are meant to experience that kind of love.

Because you deserve it.

You deserve the whole deal.
You deserve someone who reflects your mental image of true love.
You deserve someone who will love you for everything you are and for everything you want to be.
You deserve someone who goes out of their way to make it obvious that they want you in their lives.
You deserve the man who gives you their affection, commitment, time and effort, without you ever having to ask for it.
You deserve someone who takes pride in your authenticity and values you for your dreams.

You deserve lifelong, unwavering love built on both passion and true friendship. You deserve love that will feel simple and right.

Yes, you deserve it.

Despite all the heartbreaks, rejections, pain and years of conditioning that have clouded the brilliance of your soul and made you doubt your worthiness, you will break free and **believe-**

"Yes, I deserve that kind of love."

And when you believe, magic happens.

This 60 day workbook is simply a journey towards that moment of believing.

PREFACE, a.k.a THE THREE QUESTIONS

Why am I still single? How are all my friends finding love and getting married? Why do dates leave me feeling so dissatisfied? Why do I attract the same kind of people over and over? Am I asking for too much? Does the person I want even exist? Am I not attractive enough? What's wrong with me? Oh, I know.. too many romantic movies. Screw you, Netflix! I need to get real.

If similar thoughts have been frequenting your mind, you really do need to get real. And your reality simply is-

YOU DESERVE WHAT YOUR HEART DESIRES. EVERY SINGLE THING.

You can manifest a <u>blissfully happy, soul-satisfying, lifelong relationship</u> with the exact kind of person you daydream about.

If the above sentence makes you want to rage tweet @uberhype, I totally get it. You've heard that a thousand times. You know Katie manifested her dream job and Amy manifested her cute husband, a 10,000 sq. ft. single-family, a convertible and three Shih Tzus. You've been bombarded with so many manifestation stories that you've started to suspect it works.

BUT DO YOU BELIEVE?

Let's for a moment imagine that you do. You do believe you can manifest anything, including the love of your life. The question now, is- do you know who you want? EXACTLY who you want?

PEOPLE WHO SUCCESSFULLY MANIFEST TRUE LOVE HAVE ANSWERS TO THESE THREE QUESTIONS (consciously or otherwise):

1. WHO exactly do they want.
2. WHAT is stopping them from finding them.
3. HOW can they find them.

BY THE END OF THIS JOURNAL, YOU WILL ALSO HAVE THE ANSWERS.

The funny thing about life is, we spend so much mental, financial and physical effort in finding and developing all things important to us- our education, careers, physical appearance and health, nutrition and overall well being. But when it comes to finding love, WE LEAVE IT TO FATE.

By not knowing exactly who we want or how to attract them into our lives, we are left with no choice but to wait for love to randomly show up. We pray for our soulmate to appear, while constantly living in fear that we may never find them or end up with the wrong person and live an unfulfilled life.

But we're not completely wrong. Finding true love does APPEAR to be random and people finding it do APPEAR to be plain lucky. It's hard to believe that we are in any control of the manifestation of true love in our lives, let alone orchestrate it. That's because love is the one area we only own 50% of. And because we don't have full control, we let it run on auto-pilot.

Here's the thing- the moment you decide to take control of the half that belongs to you, you start attracting the other half. That's what people who seem to find true love in the most remarkable manner are doing behind the scenes. They are consciously or subconsciously manifesting it with all their hearts and souls.

PSST... IT"S NOT RANDOM

The moment you know EXACTLY who you want, you WILL start attracting them. The moment you BELIEVE you DESERVE that person, you WILL start attracting them. The moment you love yourself for ALL parts of you, you WILL start attracting that exact kind of love.

THIS JOURNAL WILL HELP YOU REACH THAT MOMENT.

This journal came to you providentially. And you took a chance on it. Since you already did that, maybe it's time to take another chance- on a journey to discover answers to the three questions that summarize your struggle with finding true love.

GIVE IT AN HONEST SHOT. YOU HAVE NOTHING TO LOSE. ONLY LIFE ALTERING INSIGHTS TO FIND AND THE LOVE OF YOUR LIFE TO MANIFEST INTO REALITY.

BY THE END OF THIS JOURNAL YOU WILL:

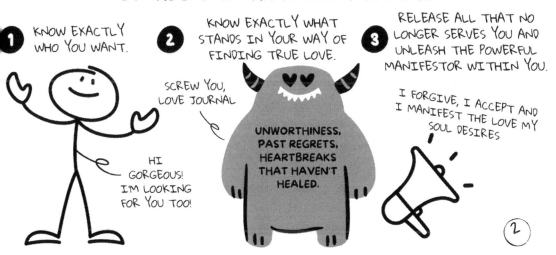

1 KNOW EXACTLY WHO YOU WANT.

2 KNOW EXACTLY WHAT STANDS IN YOUR WAY OF FINDING TRUE LOVE.

3 RELEASE ALL THAT NO LONGER SERVES YOU AND UNLEASH THE POWERFUL MANIFESTOR WITHIN YOU.

SCREW YOU, LOVE JOURNAL

HI GORGEOUS! I'M LOOKING FOR YOU TOO!

UNWORTHINESS, PAST REGRETS, HEARTBREAKS THAT HAVEN'T HEALED.

I FORGIVE, I ACCEPT AND I MANIFEST THE LOVE MY SOUL DESIRES

INTRODUCTION, a.k.a WHY THIS JOURNAL?

In my freshman year in high school, I fell in love. He wasn't a very popular guy. He was not considered traditionally good looking either. I think it was his mysterious personality that drew me in. He was the "introvert, but quite the charmer" type, the one that keeps to his group of three guy friends laughing and high-fiving sitting in a corner in the cafeteria for reasons completely unfathomable to an unassuming passerby. That passerby, who in the deadliest secret world of her adolescent heart was absolutely head over heels in love with him. And completely invisible to him.

Now, going by the acceptable high school dating code of early 2000s, a girl must NEVER approach a guy (last I heard, nothing much has changed since). She must send him hints through common friends, then wait for him to walk up to her and say hi. I spent sleepless nights thinking if I should talk to someone about it.

A word here about my looks in high school, because how I looked was the only factor that determined if my message will be reciprocated or die a painful death and enter the gossip circle from high school hell.

I was going through a bit of a self discovery phase. I *always* tied my curly, unruly hair in a tight bun and *always* had an oily layer of cold cream slathered on my face. Because I had dry skin, I thought that gave my face a sexy glow. I bought jars of my favorite brand, disregarding all of my sweet, anxious mother's concerns masquerading as friendly suggestions of how I looked so pretty just the "way you are".

Did I send a message? I did. Did it get reciprocated? It didn't. Did it enter the gossip hall of fame? Surprisingly, no. I was devastated. Not only because of the rejection. I was doubly devastated because it had made absolutely no difference to anyone. It wasn't even a rejection. It was blatant disregard.

Sending that message was the most courageous, honest and vulnerable thing I had ever done in my life. My love was a ship sunk before its maiden journey. And it sank silently.

I have vivid memories of crying on my way home from school. I have memories of watching him go steady with a sweet and pretty girl until the end of high school. I have not seen him or heard about him since then. But he kept creeping up in my dreams for many years, as that extra character who has nothing much to contribute to the story line, sometimes as that passenger on the wrong bus I get on to, looking at me silently, eyes full of judgment, or that student I momentarily cross in the hallway while I rush naked to the exam hall to write a paper I didn't know was scheduled and have not prepared for. (3)

Looking back, my first "love" experience was not all that bad. Nothing drastic happened as a consequence of me baring my heart out. But it loomed. This seemingly irrelevant experience hung low on my life for many years, germinating under the radar while I went on living oblivious to my broken heart, my crumbling confidence and my disintegrating sense of self worth.

I started repeating patterns. I would like someone and suddenly get a feeling that they are too good for me. And because my worth was slipping drastically in my own eyes, I subconsciously started believing that any guy "worth his salt" would not show any of the characteristics I showed when I fell in love in high school- he will not be needy, he won't be eager to please, eager to express his feelings, he won't be too attention giving. And sadly, he won't be attracted to me right away. Any guy who showed any of these characteristics dropped down many points in my eligibility list. Suddenly, I was the bitch. Who wasn't even pretty.

Through my early twenties, I was deep in a phase of 'bad boy syndrome'. I only liked guys who didn't like me or didn't think much of me. Sometimes those who didn't even see me. While rejecting two really nice guys- guys whose wives are extremely lucky to have found them and who I wish only the best in life.

I would love to tell you that I woke up one morning, slapped myself across the face and pulled myself out of this cycle of self sabotage. But I didn't.

However, I did find something closest to that miracle. I found a friend who kept a journal. This friend of mine, let's call her Jenny, started writing as a way of venting out her anger at her dad who she held responsible for her parents' divorce. I learnt from Jenny that she felt good when she wrote about all the hurt she felt. Because we didn't have TikTok then, it took Jenny many months before she realized that writing positively about her dad actually made her hurt less and writing about forgiving her dad made the burden she carried for two decades completely vanish, in her words- "this works as good as pot!"

This is where I wish I told you- "And that's when I took on writing as a life altering journey that set me free". But I didn't. I said to Jenny "Wow this is amazing! Maybe I can try writing in a journal." Then I forgot about it and kept living my shitty life.

It wasn't until I was 32, single, with absolutely zero self confidence to spare and getting bitter with the Universe, completely believing that I'm always singled out and that God loves to see me struggle, that I finally decided to start working on myself. And the only way I knew was to write.

I made lists. Lots and lots of them. Lists that finally revealed to me the debilitating effect my infatuation in school still had on me. Lists that made me recognize many more patterns from the past that made me feel unrecognized abandoned and worthless. I wrote lists about what I wanted from life and what had to offer. I made lists that made me angry about how I had led myself on this path. And also lists that allowed me to forgive, accept and love myself for all that I had done, not done and come to be in the process. And I finally made lists recognizing my self sabotaging patterns in love, lists that allowed me to be vulnerable and honest about what I really want in a man irrespective of my perceived worthiness of that man and lists of what's stopping me from meeting him. I was finally setting myself free.

I met my husband within a year of making those lists. And he is exactly what wished him to be. In that one year, I trained myself to mold my thoughts and educated myself on the power of scripting. I took therapy and spent a substantial amount on life coaching. But it was all worth it.

I finally manifested the man I was destined to be with and started living the life I had always desired.

If I had to summarize that one year, it would boil down to two extremely powerful processes- writing indiscriminately about my feelings and being grateful. I have come to realize that these are the only two things one needs to do to release themselves of their mental stories and blockages and achieve anything they want in life. One doesn't even need to believe in this process. They just need to do it, fake it if they will. Before they know it, they will start believing and re-writing their stories.

This journal is a blueprint of that process. It's an organized collection of all the groundwork I did to manifest the exact man I desired. I have done my best to replicate my strategy in the form of activities, prompts and reflections based on CBT techniques and Law of Attraction principles.

Are there any similarities in your current life situation with my story? Are you too becoming the kind of person who:
1. Always seems to meet or date the wrong people?
2. Struggles to find intimate love that lasts?
3. Is scared to spend the rest of their life looking for their soulmate?
4. Is scared to be alone forever?
5. Seems to be attracting people with similar characteristics?
6. Struggles generally with the idea of manifesting their desires by changing their thoughts?

If Yes, you're holding the journal that has the potential to change the direction of your life and propel you towards the love of your deepest desires.

The goal of this journal is for you to allow yourself to be loved. It exists to help you believe that you can attract and manifest your soulmate even while life keeps throwing shit your way. Believing is the toughest part of the entire manifestation process. I still struggle with it, especially when things are going wrong in life. But with practicing manifestation for so many years, I have found some belief hacks that are shared and implemented here. Trust me, these hacks work!

Lastly, I want you to know that I believe in you and your journey. In all you have within you- I believe in the empty feeling in your heart. I believe in your desire to find true love, even while you question if you will ever find it. I believe in your efforts to be a better person. And I believe in your awesomeness.

Rachel

YOU DESERVE TO BE WANTED.
YOU DESERVE LOVE THAT IS CERTAIN.
A LOVE THAT'S UNCOMPLICATED.
STABLE. CONSISTENT.
YOU DESERVE SOMEONE
THAT IS SURE OF YOU,
THAT YOU'RE SURE OF.

TRUE LOVE READINESS QUIZ

Answer the following true and false questions by circling the response that feels most applicable for you.

1. I am confident I will meet the love of my life very soon.

   O TRUE   O FALSE

2. I have a clear picture in my mind of the person I'm looking for- from physical attributes to values, personality traits and likes & dislikes.

   O TRUE   O FALSE

3. I am over my past relationship(s) and feel ready to embrace a new chapter in my life.

   O TRUE   O FALSE

4. I believe someone will be lucky to have me as their life partner.

   O TRUE   O FALSE

5. I often think about my ex(es).

   O TRUE   O FALSE

6. Generally, I think more about my past than my present or my future.

   O TRUE   O FALSE

7. When I'm alone, I usually do things I enjoy and I'm passionate about.

   O TRUE   O FALSE

8. I am confident that I will end up with the right person.

   O TRUE   O FALSE

9. I am increasingly tending to avoid going out with friends who are in a relationship.

  O TRUE   O FALSE

10. I believe the Universe has my back and will send me everything I deeply desire.

  O TRUE   O FALSE

SCORING: For Questions 1, 2, 3, 4, 7, 8, 10- Give yourself 5 points for every TRUE answer and 2 points for every FALSE answer.
For Questions 5, 6, 9- Give yourself 2 points for every TRUE answer and 5 points for every FALSE answer.

41-50: You are on your way to manifesting your one true love! Congratulations on seeing yourself for the amazing person you are and being confident in knowing that your perfect match in on their way!

31-40: Keep it up! You are on your way to believing that you deserve exactly the person your heart desires. You are kind and compassionate towards yourself and that will reflect in the relationship you are manifesting!

21-30: Continue to challenge yourself to be more compassionate and kind towards yourself. Knowing your worth is the most important step in truly believing you deserve what you desire.

20: Keep learning and moving forward knowing that self-worth can be cultivated, thoughts can be molded and the person you desire can be manifested. If millions of people can do it, so can you, no matter where you stand right now. All you need is to reach that one moment of liberation of all that stands in the way of you and your true love. And you will reach that moment, I promise!

YOU DESERVE SOMEONE
WHO REPLIES FAST.
YOU DESERVE SOMEONE WHO
NEVER GETS TIRED OF
YOUR POINTLESS STORIES.
YOU DESERVE SOMEONE WHO
WILL SHOW THEIR EAGERNESS TO TALK
TO YOU ANYTIME YOU CALL.
YOU DESERVE SOMEONE WHO WILL
MAKE YOU THEIR PRIORITY.

-unknown author

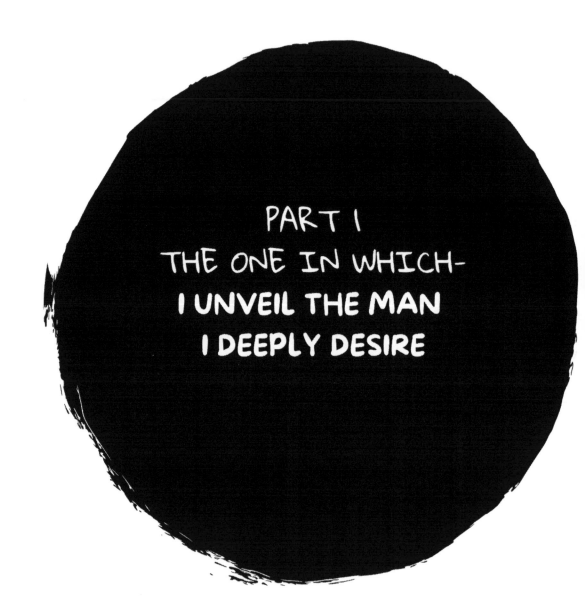

PART 1
THE ONE IN WHICH-
I UNVEIL THE MAN
I DEEPLY DESIRE

Welcome to the most exciting part of the journal. Within the pages of this chapter lies your canvas. This is where you finally reveal to yourself the exact person you are looking for. This is where he manifests in your thoughts. This is where your first accurate intention is created for the universe to fulfill.

When it comes to knowing what love is, you've had no dearth of information. Layers and layers of data have piled up on your subconscious mind about "the perfect guy"- years of exposure to pop culture, the relationships your friends have had, your own past relationships and the deep reservoir of social media have shaped an overall idea in your mind of what a life partner should or should not be. There is so much information that the lines have blurred between the "perfect guy" as a concept you've absorbed and the actual man that is right for you, the man that is made for the person you are and the man your soul deeply desires. The two are often confused, and although the two may have similarities, the man that is made for you can only be yours. His is the only kind of love that will satisfy your soul and help you grow into the best version of yourself.

You may have had fleeting images of that man. You may also have a few "non-negotiables" about him. And you definitely have a long list of things you "ABSOLUTELY DO NOT WANT" in your life partner. Now is when you find out what you "ABSOLUTELY DO WANT".

NEGATIVES ARE POSITIVES: THE UNIVERSE'S BIZARRE RECEIVING SYSTEM

\overset{DAY}{1} THE UNDESIRABLES

It's easy to know what we don't want. Because our lives will be miserable if we end up with the wrong person, we constantly think in terms of avoiding the undesirable. Always being on alert, our energies go towards finding and filtering men we don't want.

THAT ENERGY GETS SENT TO THE UNIVERSE. Not your words, not your theories about who you desire, not even your internal dialogues. The ONLY thing the universe cares about is receiving your energy frequency. If your energy frequency is mostly focused on the undesirable, the undesirable gets manifested in your life. Again and again and again.

LET'S GET THE UNDESIRABLES OUT OF THE WAY.

Let's acknowledge and accept all your thoughts about what you don't want in your life partner. This is the ONLY time we will focus on the undesirables, so they can be packed up and kept away for good.

Here's a list of attributes in a man that will make me pull my hair out and run away to an undisclosed location:

"EVERYTHING YOU CAN IMAGINE IS REAL"

-Pablo Picasso

DAY 2 — PICTURING HIM

Below is the vision board of the physical image of your true love. Write down a list of physical attributes you want in your life partner. Feeling Creative? Draw a picture of him or paste a picture of a person that best reflects the image in your mind (magazines can help). Remember, you know deep inside what you want. I invite you to get past the mental limitations of your own worthiness of the image you create. You deserve exactly who you desire. Come back to this page regularly to remind yourself of this image or cut on the frame below and make it a part of the vision board activity on page 91.

16

DAY 3 THE LOVE STORY I'LL TELL MY GRANDKIDS

It's Christmas eve. The fire is crisp in the elegant open hearth fireplace in your cozy living room. As a delicious aroma of apple pie fills the whole house, you're taking a break, sitting under red plaid blankets with your favorite people in the world- your grandkids, finally getting to the story they asked you two days ago- "how did you and grandpa meet?". Write the story below while being in presence of emotions the thought of true love evokes in you. How did you both meet? How did you know he's the one? How has the marriage been so far and how is the love still thriving after so many years?

COFFEE AND DONUT

PERSONALITY TRAITS: When you think about your soulmate, what personality characteristics come to the forefront? Write them down on the coffee mug. Reflect on your own personality traits and write them down on the donut. The sugar packs might help.

ambitious

optimistic

patient

sensitive

introverted

confident

laid-back

sincere

organized

resourceful

extroverted

goal oriented

empathetic

focused

humble

creative

MY SOULMATE IS...

I AM...

18

How does your ideal partner treat you?

How does your ideal partner treat others?

What about your soulmate makes your heart flutter?

GOALS AND ASPIRATIONS

Being aware of and understanding your aspirations, dreams, and ambitions allow for better alignment and compatibility. When partners have compatible goals, they can provide support, encouragement, and collaboration on their individual journeys.

What are your top three goals for the next five years? Write on the summits below.

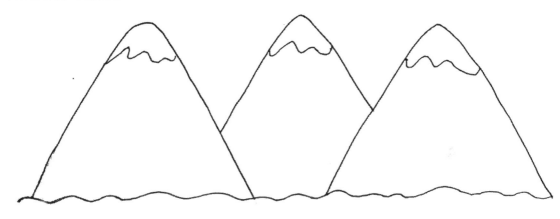

Finish this sentence:

More than anything else, before I die, I want to _____

_____

What are the top three milestones you want to achieve by the end of this year with regards to your love life (example- to meet the person and know with certainty, move in with him, get engaged, get married, travel together etc)

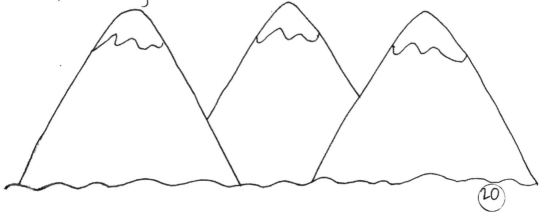

THE HAPPINESS FLOWERS

Reflect on what makes you happy. When you visualize the perfect life with your soulmate and see yourself happy, what does it entail? How can you break down the feeling of happiness into smaller feelings that are more observable? In short, what does happiness mean to you? Write in the petals below.

HAPPINESS IN GENERAL IS...

HAPPINESS IN LOVE IS...

21

SHINE A LIGHT ON THAT: Do you sometimes feel there is so much more to you than what meets the eye of the average date? Do you feel that relationships with some men end before they can see your true worth? What qualities in you have remained under the wraps in the past, qualities that make you stand apart but are not too noticeable upfront? Write them down below.

THINGS ABOUT ME I INTEND TO SHINE A LIGHT ON:

A SHARED LIFE

SHARED VALUES: Shared values are pivotal to the success of a relationship, and while we may be aware of ours, we sometimes overlook the values we are looking for in our ideal partner. With shared values, you are more likely to be aligned with your partner in your beliefs, priorities, and decision-making processes. Let's explore the values you are looking for in your soulmate and the ones you bring to the relationship.

MY IDEAL PARTNER'S VALUES	MY VALUES
CORE VALUES: Fundamental beliefs and principles that guide a person's behavior and decision-making.	
FAMILY AND RELATIONSHIP VALUES: These values reflect how you and your partner prioritize and nurture your relationship, as well as your approach to building a family if that is a shared goal.	
PERSONAL GROWTH AND SELF IMPROVEMENT VALUES: These include personal growth, continuous learning, and self-improvement.	

 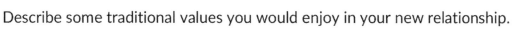

DAY 10   A SHARED LIFE

Describe some traditional values you would enjoy in your new relationship.

Describe some alternative or unusual values you would appreciate.

How spiritual is your soulmate and what are their spiritual beliefs like?

Having common interests with your partner can contribute to increased happiness and fulfillment in life. Make a list of interests, passions and hobbies that you want to share with your soulmate.

While unconditional love lays the foundation for a lifelong relationship, there are other practical factors to consider to make a marriage or relationship thrive. There is no shame or inherent wrongness in seeking a life partner who is financially stable, earns well, or pursues a specific career field. When it comes to choosing a life partner, compatibility in various aspects, including financial matters, is a valid consideration.

Each individual has the right to prioritize qualities that are important to them in a partner, and financial stability can be one such consideration. If it's yours, allow yourself to be completely non-judgemental and write about it using the present tense. Only when you declare what you want will the universe be able to deliver to you. I urge you to be as specific as you've been in describing other aspects you're seeking in your life partner. If you don't have specific expectations on any of the below categories, try writing what matters to you instead.

MY IDEAL PARTNER'S FIELD OF WORK:

MY IDEAL PARTNER'S FINANCIAL SITUATION AND INCOME:

MY IDEAL PARTNER'S HOUSING SITUATION:

MY IDEAL PARTNER'S MINDSET ABOUT MONEY:

Physical compatibility, including sexual compatibility, is important for maintaining a satisfying and fulfilling relationship. It involves a mutual understanding of each other's desires, preferences, and needs, which allows for a harmonious and enjoyable physical relationship. Physical intimacy and compatibility contribute to a sense of closeness, passion, and satisfaction, enhancing the overall quality and longevity of the relationship.

When you envision your ideal relationship, what is the intimacy like? How do you and your partner express physical affection? How is the sexual chemistry and connection between you and your soulmate?

How does your soulmate show they love you?

FAMILY DYNAMICS AND SOCIAL INTERACTIONS

The experiences, values, and communication patterns learned within the family shape one's understanding of relationships and influence their behavior and expectations in intimate partnerships.

What are their family dynamics like?

Describe their friendships and social skills.

What things does your ideal partner do to be thoughtful of you and others?

If getting married and/or starting a family with your soulmate is something you desire, visualizing details related to your wedding and your life as a married couple can be groundbreaking in raising the vibrations of your thoughts. By visualizing these details, you can tap into your emotions and align your thoughts and actions with the future you envision.

Visualize your dream wedding with your soulmate and describe the following aspects of your wedding day. Try to focus on the feelings and emotions associated with the event, along with specific details if you desire. By visualizing the essence and emotions of your ideal wedding, you open yourself up to a range of possibilities and allow the universe to bring you a manifestation that may exceed your expectations.

Emotional Atmosphere: Describe the emotional atmosphere of your wedding, such as the love, joy, and happiness shared between you and your partner, as well as the warmth and support of your loved ones.

Ceremony Setting: Describe the setting for your ceremony, whether it's a picturesque outdoor location, a romantic chapel or place of worship, or any other venue that resonates with you. Picture the decorations, flowers, and any unique elements that reflect your personal style and values.

Exchange of Vows: Imagine yourselves standing at the altar, exchanging heartfelt vows that express your love, commitment, and shared vision for the future. Visualize and describe the emotions you and your partner are experiencing in this special moment.

Celebration: Picture the reception and celebration that follows the ceremony. Visualize and describe the ambiance, music, dancing, and all the elements that make the celebration memorable and enjoyable for you and your guests.

MY DREAM HONEYMOON: Describe below the dream destination for your honeymoon. Visualize the quality time you and your partner will have on your honeymoon. Picture yourselves enjoying intimate moments, deep conversations, and shared laughter. Describe below the connection and love that will deepen during this special time together.

MY HAPPILY EVER AFTER

What are the ingredients that will go into your ultimate "Happily Ever After" potion? Write the words, feelings, things or emotions that you are inviting into your life right now.

DASH OF-

SPRINKLE OF-

SMIDGEN OF-

FEATHER OF-

HINT OF-

PETAL OF-

SPRIG OF-

BAG OF-

SPLASH OF-

SLIVER OF-

30

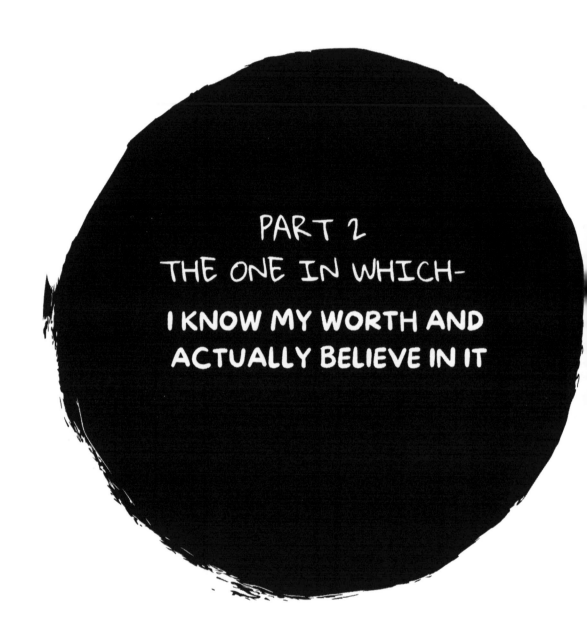

PART 2
THE ONE IN WHICH-

I KNOW MY WORTH AND
ACTUALLY BELIEVE IN IT

Life without our soulmate can seem unfulfilled. True unconditional love makes us feel complete, enriches our life with joy and beauty and gives our soul a sense of fulfillment. We all want that kind of pure, unadulterated love. The love in which we are accepted, cherished and celebrated for every atom of our being. No wonder, the pursuit of that love becomes an obsession and the elusiveness of it can often leave a big hole in our lives. It's almost impossible to be truly happy, to enjoy small joys of life, to even sit in the stillness of the present moment when we operate from a lack of love. Deep within our hearts, we long for the love of our life to mirror our soul, that man who will kiss us and say- "I have been looking for you too".

Attracting that love is simple and follows a Universal Law. Note that it's a LAW, not a PROBABILITY; similar to the Laws of Motion, meaning that it will work the same way each time. However, just like the Laws of Motion can get skewed in vacuum or on another planet, the Universal Law of Attraction can show skewed results under certain circumstances. These circumstances are: not being authentic about what one wants, being stuck in past regrets and mistakes, trauma and heartbreaks that haven't healed, feeling unworthy of the things we desire and somewhere deep down being comfortable in our present state (for a fear of the unknown).

If you have tried and failed at manifestation and declared the Universal Law to be unpredictable and complicated, you may be operating from one or more of the above mentioned circumstances. It's simple- the moment you identify your situation and despite that, decide to operate from a position of faith, you will see that the Law always works and you will believe in the true power of your thoughts to attract and manifest in flesh and blood the love of your life. And when you believe, you will start seeing miracles not only in love, but in all areas of you life. But how will you do that?

How will you believe? The answer is- you will not. Not now, that is. You will only pretend. While you work on removing the circumstances that block manifestation, you will pretend to believe. As the circumstances clear, you will feel no more need to pretend. That is when you truly believe.

In the next few pages, you will embark on a journey of deep personal awareness, inner healing, forgiveness and gratitude, changes in thought and belief patterns and reinstating a compassionate, loving relationship with yourself. Because your internal world creates your outer world, let's fill your inner world with the joy, abundance and pure love you were always meant to embody.

HEALING YOUR LIMITING BELIEFS ABOUT LOVE

Do you sometimes feel that you live in two different realities? The reality of surface level knowledge and the reality of feeling emotions that are completely inverse of that knowledge? For example- you may know that negative thoughts will only lead you to attract more of that negativity. But at the face of a flood of negative, self depreciating thoughts you may stand helpless, day after day, unable to use that knowledge in any way.

THE CYCLE OF SELF FULFILLING PROPHECIES: Limiting beliefs about anything are conceived at the first experience of negativity. Your limiting beliefs about love started the first time you felt rejection in love, maybe as a young girl.

Adolescent years are the most vulnerable in a young girl's life. Negative experiences that occur at this age get embedded deep within our minds and if we lack a strong support system to help us resolve that negativity, the hold of that experience gets even stronger. If you were to face the same rejection or heartbreak today, it will not be so life altering, so devastating. Looking back, the rejection you faced may be mild as compared to more that came later in life.

But the hold of that rejection on your subconscious mind is the strongest. The inner child in you needs assurance, sympathy and most importantly- love. She needs a voice of reason who will assure her of her worthiness and give her the hope for the future she most desperately needs. But doesn't receive.

And because she never receives it, her hurt from the rejection turns into fear. Fear of being rejected again. She started out with a blank slate. But the first major rejection sets the tone for the story that followed. The first seeds of the belief that men are not truthful, trustworthy or that she is not "good enough" for a good looking, popular, smart, loving or _____ (fill in your word) guy were sown.

The longer she held on to those beliefs, the stronger the beliefs got and the more she manifested similar experiences. Her limiting beliefs about love placed her in patterns she couldn't seem to explain. All of a sudden she's started repeating the exact same cycle and in the process started wondering if real love will ever be possible for her.

THE GIFT OF HOPE: The most remarkable quality of the human experience is hope. No matter how bad things are, there is always a tiny flame of hope burning deep within. You may say "I have no hope I will ever find true love", but somewhere within you, the hope that true love will find you, never dies. That tiny flame is powerful enough to pull you out of the cycle of self fulfilling prophecies.

WHAT LIES BENEATH

On the part of the iceberg visible above water, write words/phrases that best describe how people see you. This is your outer world. On the part that's under the surface, write words/phrases that best describe your dominant emotions deep within. This is your inner world. Reflect on what you write. Are your outer and inner worlds completely at odds? Or do they mostly overlap? This reflection will give you an idea on the reasons why manifestation may not be working for you. You may be trying to send out frequencies that don't have a vibrational match with your inner state of being.

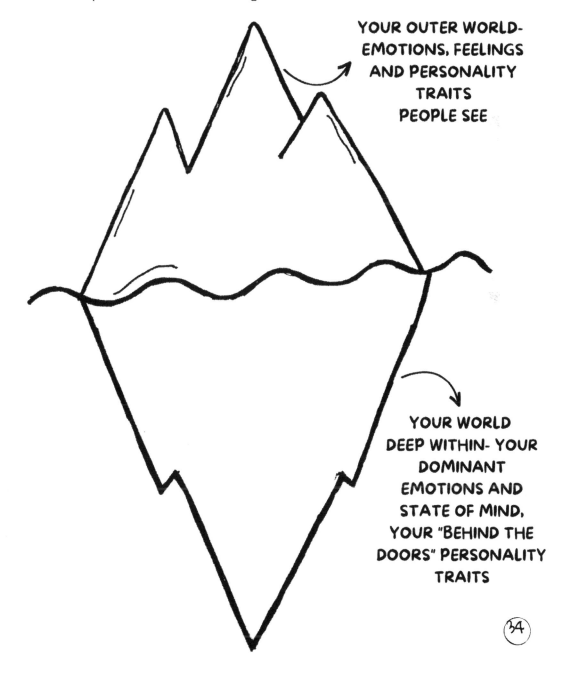

YOUR OUTER WORLD- EMOTIONS, FEELINGS AND PERSONALITY TRAITS PEOPLE SEE

YOUR WORLD DEEP WITHIN- YOUR DOMINANT EMOTIONS AND STATE OF MIND, YOUR "BEHIND THE DOORS" PERSONALITY TRAITS

MY FIRST REAL, TERRIFYING, DEVASTATING HEARTBREAK

Think back to your first real heartbreak. What exactly happened? Write as if you're telling your story to a friend.

How did that experience make you feel? Circle all the words/phrases that reflect your emotions in that experience, or write your own.

- DEEP SADNESS
- A SENSE OF LOSS
- SHAME
- DISAPPOINTMENT
- LONELINESS
- ANGER AT YOURSELF
- ANGER AT THE OTHER PERSON
- SELF DOUBT
- RESENTMENT
- EMBARRASMENT
- PERCEIVING REJECTION AS UNFAIR
- CONFUSION BECAUSE OF MIXED SIGNALS
- UNWORTHY

_____

_____

_____

_____

_____

_____

_____

Looking back, what lessons do you think seeped into your subconscious mind as a result of the heartbreak and abandonment you faced? What decisions do you think you made based on the lessons you learnt?

LESSONS AND DECISIONS FROM MY DEVASTATING HEARTBREAK-

Now, imagine that your best friend, or someone you love unconditionally had the exact experience of heartbreak as you and tells you exactly what you've written. What would you tell her about the lessons she learnt and the burden of which she is about to carry through her life?

A LETTER TO MY YOUNGER SELF

Be in awareness of the emotions you felt during your first major heartbreak. Imagine walking back home one day and finding a letter addressed to you- a letter of compassion, love, hope and encouragement- from yourself in the future. Fill in the blanks to the guided self-compassion letter below and imagine posting it to your younger self. In the eye of your mind, imagine finding and reading this letter during those hard days.

Dear _____

(YOUR NAME HERE)

I know you have gone through a lot lately. I want you to know that when

_____

(INSERT SITUATION)

_____

I was behind you all the way. I know you are feeling _____

(DESCRIBE HOW YOU FELT)

_____

and it's hard for you to look at the positive side of things right now because

_____

(DESCRIBE WHAT WAS DIFFICULT ABOUT THE SITUATION)

_____

All your feelings are normal and valid. I want to hug you and tell you that you are going to be okay because _____

(WHY IS IT GOING TO BE OKAY?)

_____

You are worthy of all the best things life has to offer and I promise you that things will get better. Know that this experience was a small challenge in the beautiful adventure that your future will bring. Lastly, I want you to know that I love you unconditionally and I know you will come out on the other side with

_____

(WHAT POSITIVE QUALITIES DEVELOPED IN YOU FROM THIS EXPERIENCE?)

_____

(END WITH ANYTHING ELSE YOU WANT TO SAY)

with love,

_____

(YOUR NAME HERE)

"JUMP OFF THE TRAIN OF THOUGHTS THAT DON'T TAKE YOU TO A BETTER PLACE"

-Unknown

DAY 20 THOUGHT PATTERNS

You identified in the pervious activities a few feelings that emerged with your first major experience of rejection in early love. Some of these feelings may have changed or disappeared as you had more positive experiences later in life. Some may have stayed or developed stronger with other experiences that echoed that first negative experience. Every person has 2-3 dominant feelings that stay through life that develop into a thought pattern. This thought pattern reflects in all areas of our lives. Let's find your 3 dominant thoughts that have formed a pattern. This is a two step process.

STEP 1: MY MAJOR LIFE ALTERING EXPERIENCES

Write down below and on the next page 4 (or more) important experiences you had in your life that you think shaped your personality over the years and could be standing behind your limiting beliefs. These experiences may or may not be related to your ex relationships and could be from other significant areas- parental love/support during childhood, relationship between parents, friendships, academics or work. Besides each experience, write down the dominant feeling(s) or thoughts that arose from that experience. For example- an important experience can be working really hard to make the cut for a sport in school and not getting selected. The dominant feelings/thoughts from that could be- "I am not good at anything", "I can never succeed", or feelings of defeat. Get into as much detail as you want. It's important to be descriptive about how you felt because these are the feelings/dialogs that form the core of the internal mental chatter you have today. Some experiences may seem trivial to you now, but the fact that you remember them says everything about the impact these had on you.

THE EXPERIENCE	DOMINANT FEELING(S)/THOUGHTS FROM THE EXPERIENCE

THE EXPERIENCE	DOMINANT FEELING(S)/THOUGHTS FROM THE EXPERIENCE

STEP 2 : FINDING MY DOMINANT THOUGHT PATTERN

Reflect on your responses from the previous step and circle the dominant feelings/thoughts that you've repeatedly written. The feeling/thought that has been repeated the most number of times is your #1 dominant feeling in life. Find out your #1, #2 and #3 dominant feelings from the activity on the previous page and write them in the boxes below:

MY #1 DOMINANT FEELING/THOUGHT IS:

MY #2 DOMINANT FEELING/THOUGHT IS:

MY #3 DOMINANT FEELING/THOUGHT IS:

THE 3 FEELINGS/THOUGHTS YOU'VE WRITTEN ABOVE
FORM THE CORE OF YOUR THOUGHT PATTERN IN LIFE.

Congratulations! You've completed the most important step towards liberating yourself from limiting beliefs and are now one giant leap closer to manifesting who you desire. The thought pattern above reflects in all areas of your life, including your expectations about finding true love. The story you tell yourself everyday at a deep subconscious level is soaked in these thoughts. That story finds its way into the vibrational frequency of your thoughts. As a result, patterns of that story keep manifesting in your life. And the story keeps getting stronger.

IT'S TIME TO REWRITE THAT STORY.

DAY 21 DESERVING MY DREAM MAN

Refer to pages 15, 18 and 19 where you've described the man your soul desires. How do you feel when you see your list of desires? Color the clouds that best describe your feelings, or write your own.

EMPOWERED

WORTHY

LOVED

EXCITED

ENTHUSIASTIC

OPTIMISTIC

CONFIDENT

HAPPY

ANXIOUS

HOPEFUL

THRILLED

UNSURE

NERVOUS

SCARED

INSECURE

EMBARRASSED

UNWORTHY

OVERWHELMED

HELPLESS

42

DESERVING MY DREAM MAN

Write down all the reasons why you may be feeling that way about your desires.

Do you believe that you deserve the man you've described? Write about that belief below.

THE STORIES I TELL: When friends and family ask you why you're still single, what are the reasons and stories you tell them? (examples- joking about how all the good ones are taken or that you're not ready to be in a relationship until you feel settled in some other area of life).

But if you're really honest with yourself, your love life doesn't look the way you want it to because:

It's natural to experience fear or apprehension about being in a relationship. New relationships are rooted in unpredictability and can bring about changes in our lives we may not be ready for.

You could be fearful about being emotionally vulnerable or fear the possibility of experiencing rejection, heartbreak, or betrayal. There could be concerns about losing your independence or personal freedom. It's important to explore and be aware of the fears that might be pulling you back from actively seeking and manifesting your one true love.

What are you most afraid of when it comes to relationships? Put your fears in the bubbles below. Visualize these bubbles gently flying away, taking with them all that's keeping you from embracing true love.

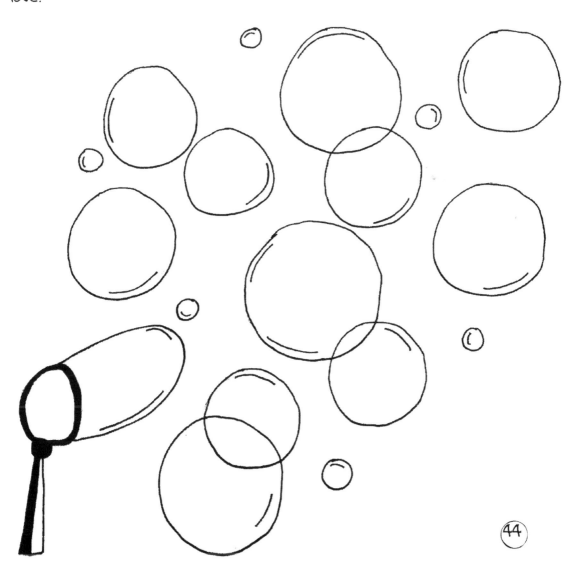

44

DO I BELIEVE IN TRUE LOVE?

A belief in true love is a strong, unwavering hope and optimism about finding a deep and meaningful connection with someone. It's a deep awareness and trust in the possibility of experiencing a profound and lasting bond with a compatible partner. This awareness often embodies a positive and hopeful outlook towards life in general.

When you think of finding true love, or when you watch deeply committed love being depicted in movies or novels, how do you feel about it? Do you disregard it as being unreal, or do you wholeheartedly believe that such love exists? Explore your beliefs below.

MY BELIEFS ABOUT TRUE LOVE

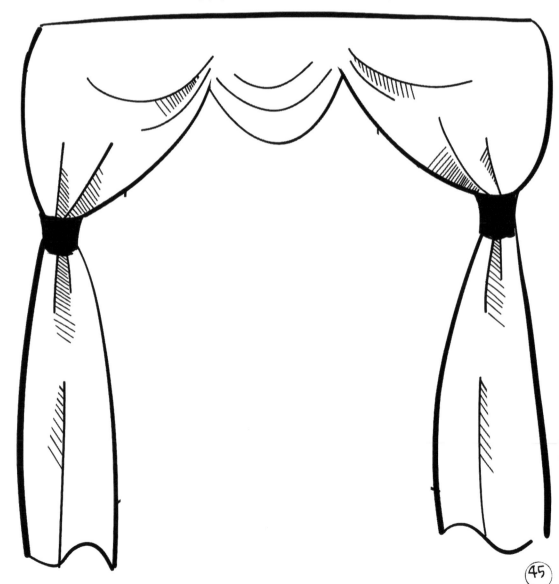

DAY 24 — PAST MISTAKES AND REGRETS IN LOVE

Regrets from past relationships are a major roadblock to manifestation of love. When we carry unresolved regrets and lingering pain from previous relationships, it can create emotional barriers that hinder our ability to imagine and manifest a fulfilling relationship.

Fear of repeating past mistakes or encountering similar pain can lead to frequencies of guardedness, hesitation, or even self-sabotage. Despite knowing what we want in our next relationship, we are unable to manifest it and instead attract more of that fear in our lives.

Do you have any regrets about actions or decisions you took in your previous relationship(s) that you wish you had taken differently? Write them down below.

How do you think being stuck in regrets and mistakes of your past relationship(s) is lowering your chances of finding true love?

When thinking about those regrets, do you look at yourself critically or compassionately? What do you say to yourself when you think about those mistakes?

Now, speak to yourself about those mistakes and regrets from a place of self-compassion and empathy. Write yourself a short letter forgiving yourself for all your past decisions and actions.

To

The

Girl

I was

Then

"FORGIVING SOMEONE
DOESN'T GIVE THEM A
FREE PASS. IT GIVES YOU
A FREE PASS TO
MOVE ON"

-Charles F. Glassman

At some point, you just have to let go and move on. At some point, you have to realize it was not meant to be. At some point, you have to forgive the pain, the disappointments, the anxiety and the people that you've been holding so tight in your mind. At some point, you have to know it's okay for things to not work out. At some point, you have to summon all your strength and be headed to a new direction because it will lead closer to your true path.

Write down all the things, emotions and people you are letting go of at this moment.

I FORGIVE AND LET GO OF...

From the sentences below, mark the ones you are likely to think or say to yourself when things go wrong in any area of life.

O Nothing good ever happens to me.
O I knew this would happen.
O I am always singled out.
O Just when things start looking up, something has to go wrong.

Do you believe that there is an unseen force that oversees your life and is meant to guide you in the right direction? Explore your beliefs about this force.

Do you trust that the force listens to your desires and answers them? What is your relationship with the force?

Reflect back to all the times you desired and asked for something and received it. Make a list of five fulfilled desires, irrespective of how substantial or trivial those were. Don't stop at five if you can think of more.

Fill in the blanks below to complete the letter of gratitude to the Universe for manifesting the desires you listed yesterday. Imagine sending it to the Universe and as the Universe receives this letter, imagine a warm golden hue entering your body, filling you with an abundance of love and peace and a feeling of oneness with the Universe.

Dear Universe,

Thank you for always being there for me, for listening to all my desires and being aware of everything I want. I am so happy and grateful that you answered my prayer when I asked for

_____

(MENTION THE DESIRES THAT GOT FULFILLED, REFER TO PREVIOUS PAGE)

_____

Sometimes, when things don't go the way I desire, I may come across as ungrateful or frustrated, but I want you to know that I trust your eternal wisdom and understand that you echo my dominant feelings and thoughts when answering my prayers.

I believe that you are always on my side. I believe that you always listen and match the frequencies of my thoughts and desires.

What I ask this time is very important to me. I want

_____

(DESCRIBE YOUR DESIRED RELATIONSHIP)

_____

_____

and I trust that it will come to manifest by

_____

(WRITE EXACT DATE)

Thank you dear Universe for filling my life with true, unconditional love and for manifesting the man of my dreams. I love you and trust you.

with love and light,

_____

(YOUR NAME HERE)

51

DAY 28   I AM ENOUGH

Here's the one and only reason why self love is absolutely critical for you:

THE RELATIONSHIP YOU HAVE WITH YOURSELF IS THE RELATIONSHIP YOU WILL HAVE WITH YOUR SOULMATE.

Self-love is vital for finding someone else to love us in a healthy and fulfilling manner. When we genuinely love and accept ourselves, we emit a positive and confident energy that naturally attracts others who align with our authentic selves. When we cultivate self-love, we attract partners who appreciate and cherish us for who we are, leading to the manifestation of true and authentic love in our lives.

What are five things you love about your personality and attitude? (examples- I am patient, a good listener, make people laugh, pleasant and friendly, hard working etc). Write in the bubbles below.

I am awesome because

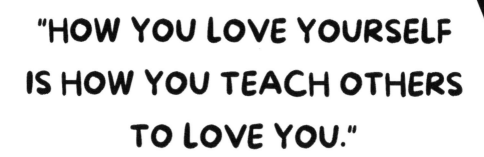

"HOW YOU LOVE YOURSELF
IS HOW YOU TEACH OTHERS
TO LOVE YOU."

-Rupi Kaur

What are five of your favorite physical attributes of yourself (yes, your left profile when you pose for a picture counts too). Make a list and do not stop at five if you remember more.

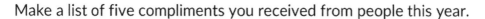

Make a list of five compliments you received from people this year.

You may think that there's nothing much unique about you, that you don't stand out in any way, but the truth cannot be further from that. Deep down, you are aware of the qualities and interests you have that are unique, that you do amazingly well, or that people ask you for help on. List one such amazing quality about you that elevates you from the rest of the crowd. Don't stop at one if you are aware of more.

DAY 31   SELF CARE

Taking care of yourself doesn't mean- "me first". It means- "me too".
Write below five things you already do everyday that make you happy.

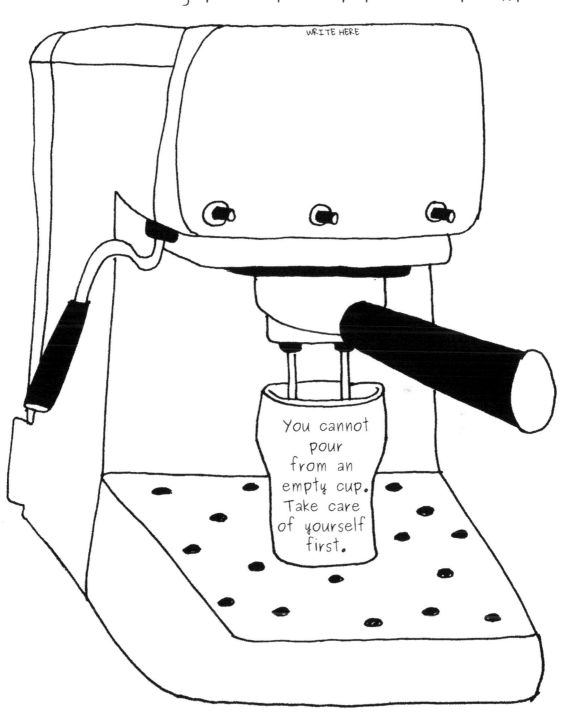

WRITE HERE

You cannot
pour
from an
empty cup.
Take care
of yourself
first.

56

DAY 32 GIVE YOURSELF PERMISSION

Self care has got a bad rap lately. Who needs another social media feed trying to sell us luxury skincare, expensive bath salt, and crystal massage wands, all in the name of self care? Self care can be about these things, and there's nothing wrong about pampering ourselves once in a while. But in essence, self care is a daily practice in which we provide our mind, body and soul the recharge it needs. Pausing in the rush of the day to drink water, moving your body, or just telling yourself its okay to feel what you're feeling is as valid in self care as settling down with a glass of wine in a warm bath. Self care is being there for others, but never leaving yourself behind.

If the idea of self care appeals to you, write down what you can do daily to care a little bit more about your body, mind, and spirit.

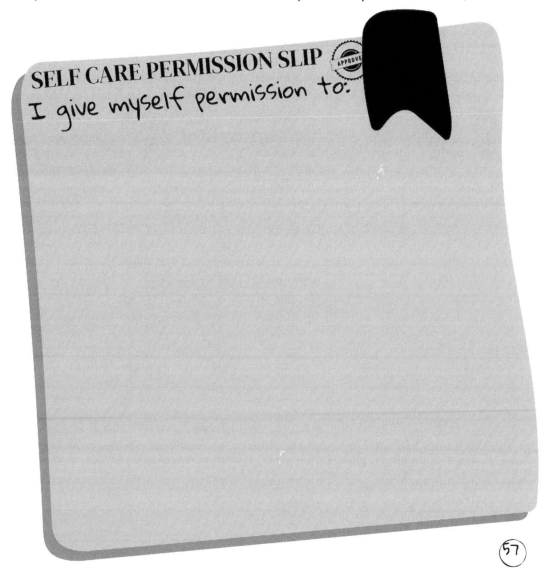

SELF CARE PERMISSION SLIP

APPROVED

I give myself permission to:

MY PROUDEST MOMENTS: In the following exercise, list down five (or more) moments in the last year that made you proud of yourself. These don't need to be of major significance or something that other people acknowledged. If you felt proud of what you did, that's all that matters.

I felt proud of myself when...

List the most important relationships in your life right now. How do they make you feel about yourself?

We all have people in our lives who are our biggest supporters. These are the people who always see the positive in us, who brighten us on our most dreary days and who provide unwavering encouragement and beliefs in our abilities. We don't even need a whole team to make us feel worthy, sometimes just one person is enough. Who is/are your biggest cheerleader(s)? How do they make you feel?

Write a few sentences thanking your cheerleader(s) for everything they do for you.

We all are hard on ourselves from time to time. But if we notice closely, we will find certain triggers that make us go down on ourselves the hardest. For example- we may let ourselves slack if we don't organize our rooms, make our beds or wash the dishes piling up in the sink. But we voice an opinion too strongly with a friend, or say no to a request by a colleague because we feel overworked, and we might suddenly get overly critical of ourselves and spiral down into a whirlpool of negative self-talk.

Reflect on the areas in which you get most critical of yourself. What situations make you go down hardest on yourself? List them here.

Imagine the best version of yourself- the one that has achieved her highest spiritual potential. What qualities does your higher self have? Write below.

What are your favorite memories from your childhood? Describe two major memories in the jars below. What were your dominant emotions during these experiences?

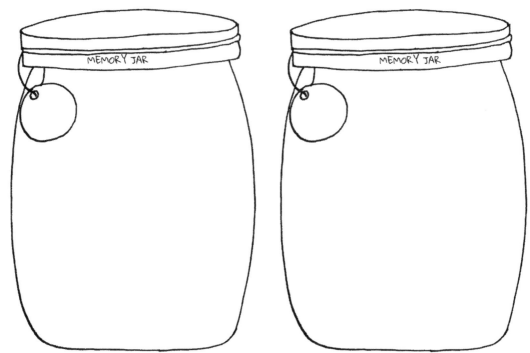

MEMORY JAR   MEMORY JAR

Reflect on one (or more) experience(s) in your adult life that evoked positive emotions similar to your favorite childhood memory. Describe the experience(s) in the balloons below.

POSITIVE "WHAT IFS"

We all worry from time to time. Some of us are chronic worriers, others not so much. In whatever category you fall, one thing doesn't change- worrying about things that we cannot control is totally futile and extremely stressful.

But you may still worry. That's because your worries are valid and important to you. Like all undesirable emotions, the emotional state of worrying needs your love and attention and a compassionate farewell. The most powerful way to do that is to write down your worries. And then rewrite them from a perspective of positivity and empowerment. Worries need to be acknowledged to be released.

Make a list of the top five things you are worried about at this stage in life, using the phrase "What if" (example- "What If I end up single?") Don't stop at five if there are more.

Now, write the opposite of each of the worry sentences you wrote above, again using the phrase "what if". (example- "What if I end up single" becomes "What if I end up in a relationship?").

Read and reflect on your positive "what if" sentences. By attaching the phrase "What If" to a positive outcome, you not only removed yourself from your original worry, you elevated yourself to see what's possible. You instantly uplifted your frequencies and shifted your mindset from doubt to hope, from lack to abundance, from fearing what may never happen, to imagining what's possible. Worries, by their nature, are not truths or facts, they are rooted in uncertainty. You can use this uncertainty to your advantage by replacing a negative uncertainty with a positive one.

"DO WHAT YOU LOVE.
AS YOU COMMIT TO YOUR
JOY, YOU WILL ATTRACT
AN AVALANCHE OF JOYFUL
THINGS."

-Rhonda Byrne

DAY 38 — PASSIONS AND INTERESTS

The simple technique behind manifestation is to be able to increase the vibrations of your thoughts to match what you desire. The vibrations of your thoughts will elevate only if your feelings and emotions resonate at a higher frequency. One way to do that is to engage in activities that make you happy.

Have you ever entered a trance-like state doing something you're passionate about? Have you lost track of time and even physical needs like thirst and hunger while being lost in an activity of interest?

Pursuing one's passions and interests is a transformative journey that can significantly contribute to happiness and self-love. There may be uncontrollable situations in life that force us to operate at a lower level of frequency, but one undeniable way to elevate ourselves, which is easy and completely under our control, is to engage in activities that we enjoy.

When life gets tough, one area of our life that gets affected the hardest can be pursuing our interests. We may not feel like finishing the crochet we started, or go on that trip to Peru, or attend that book club any more. We may think- "What's the point?"

But it's important for us. It's a simple way we can remain in touch with our higher consciousness. It is also a way we can strengthen our self image, increase our self confidence and remain true to our uniqueness.

What are your true passions and interests? Make a list below.

At this stage in life, are you actively pursuing the above listed passions? If not, explore the reasons below.

Are you pushing off any passions or interests for after you find your true love? If yes, which ones are those?

If your answer to the above question was 'yes', explore the reasons why you feel you can enjoy those passions only after you've found true love.

Imagine already being with your one true love and sharing a beautiful, fulfilled life with him. Will there be any changes in the way you're approaching your passions and interests now? Write about the changes below.

What is that one passion or interest that you want to restart or continue this year? If the idea of pursuing your passion interests you, make a list of three things you can do right away to rekindle that hobby/interest.

PART 3
THE ONE IN WHICH—
I MANIFEST TRUE LOVE

GRATITUDE YIELDS TRUE LOVE

Gratitude forms the essential foundation for finding true love in life. When we cultivate a genuine sense of gratitude, we shift our focus to appreciate and value the present moment, the people in our lives, and the experiences we encounter.

This mindset of gratitude enables us to approach relationships with an open heart. Gratitude cultivates a positive and optimistic outlook, attracting more love and abundance into our lives. Gratitude is the single tool that elevates frequencies instantly and can align your thoughts with your highest self, the self of yours that lives in synchronicity with the universe.

Despite the fact that a mindset of gratitude is so easy to implement in life, we struggle with it, and reasonably so. Afterall, when we are so far away from what we want, how can we shake the sadness away and step into gratitude? Here's how.

Gratitude will wipe out all negative emotions. You don't have to feel positive emotions to feel gratitude. Instead, you can use gratitude as a tool to foster positive emotions within you. If you're spending time getting yourself out of sadness, you're focusing on sadness and only attracting more of it in your life. To remove sadness, you practice gratitude. You practice and practice until you're really happy. Gratitude is so powerful in changing your life that you have to only practice it for a few days before you start seeing a shift in sadness. Gratitude shifts your perspective from nothing to everything. It shows you are enough.

Gratitude is the easiest and fastest way to change your life. Gratitude is acknowledging and being grateful for everything you have and are receiving every single day. As you practice it more, you will feel your whole body softening and relaxing. You will feel a sense of relief, as if something is releasing from your body. As you practice this extremely simple exercise, you are letting go of negativity.

Gratitude makes us happy. It's as simple as that. It's the greatest power you have to change your life. The key is to be grateful for everything, no matter how small it is (you can be grateful for the air you're breathing, for waking up to see another morning or for having clean water to drink. It all counts).

It may seem simple, it might be something you've heard a million times. You may be tempted to skip this step and go to the more "meaty" parts ahead. You may think the following exercise is rudimentary. You may think there is nothing in your life to be really grateful for right now. Or, you may think "I'm already grateful for a lot of things, I don't need to do this exercise."

I humbly urge you not to skip this step. Writing is extremely powerful. You may reluctantly start writing a line and before you know, you're filling up the page. You're feeling strangely happy, and you don't know why. Gratitude will truly shift frequencies of your thoughts and empower you to function as your truest self.

The Practice of Gratitude:
This is a 21 day exercise, but you're welcome to continue it in a blank journal or notebook thereafter. The next 21 pages are designed for you to affirm to the Universe your intentions of manifesting true love in your life. Start each day's affirmations with the practice of gratitude. Each day, you can be grateful for the same or different things, big or small things, a person or an experience, it doesn't matter.

MY 21 DAY BELIEF BOOTCAMP

This belief bootcamp is designed to reprogram your subconscious mind into believing. Believing that you deserve the exact vision of love you created through the pages of this workbook, believing that you're letting go of all that doesn't serve your highest purpose in life, and believing that NOW is your time to receive miracles beyond your wildest imagination.

For the next 21 days, start with writing about what you're grateful for. Follow it up with scripting your day's affirmations for the universe to manifest.

Writing is a very powerful tool. Each word you write and repeat gets imprinted permanently into your subconscious mind, allowing the Universe to reflect it back into in your life as a real feeling, thought or person.

As you write each printed affirmation 6 times, you're transforming your vibrations to align in synchronicity with the universe, enabling a chain of events to occur to lead you to exactly what you desire.

SO, ARE YOU READY TO MEET THE LOVE OF YOUR LIFE?
HERE WE GO...

"ACKNOWLEDGING THE GOOD
THAT YOU ALREADY HAVE
IN YOUR LIFE
IS THE FOUNDATION
OF ALL ABUNDANCE."

-Eckhart Tolle

Today, I am happy and grateful for: *Date:* _____

_____

_____

_____

_____

TRUSTING THE PROCESS
"I trust the timing of my life."

_____

_____

_____

_____

_____

_____

"I am exactly where I'm meant to be."

_____

_____

_____

_____

_____

"I trust. I believe. I receive."

_____

_____

_____

_____

_____

DAY 40 RELEASING OLD BURDENS

Today, I am happy and grateful for: *Date:* _____

_____
_____
_____
_____

(WRITE YOUR THREE DOMINANT THOUGHTS FROM PAGE 41 FOR THIS AFFIRMATION)

"I lovingly release _____, _____, and _____"

_____
_____
_____
_____
_____

"I release all that no longer serves my higher good."

_____
_____
_____
_____
_____

"I clear away old patterns and beliefs."

_____
_____
_____
_____
_____

LETTING GO

Today, I am happy and grateful for: *Date:* _____

_____

_____

_____

_____

"I let go of fear, worry, anger, and blame."

_____

_____

_____

_____

_____

"I support my deepest healing."

_____

_____

_____

_____

_____

**"As I change my thoughts,
the world around me changes."**

_____

_____

_____

_____

_____

DAY 42 FREEING MYSELF

Today, I am happy and grateful for: *Date:* _____

_____
_____
_____
_____

"I observe negative feelings, and let them pass."

_____
_____
_____
_____
_____

"I free myself from fear of the unknown."

_____
_____
_____
_____

"I have let go of my past and am ready to give and receive an abundance of love."

_____
_____
_____
_____
_____

Today, I am happy and grateful for: Date: _____

_____

_____

_____

_____

"I am patient and gentle with myself
as I'm in the midst of transformation. "

_____

_____

_____

_____

_____

"I release self-criticism and choose self-love."

_____

_____

_____

_____

"I let go of all limiting beliefs and replace them
with love, hope and peace."

_____

_____

_____

_____

_____

Today, I am happy and grateful for: Date: _____

_____

_____

_____

_____

"I release all criticisms towards myself and forgive."

_____

_____

_____

_____

_____

"I forgive those who have wronged me and choose to live a life full of love, joy and peace."

_____

_____

_____

_____

_____

"I step away from the prison of resentment into freedom."

_____

_____

_____

_____

_____

_____

Today, I am happy and grateful for: Date: _____

_____

_____

_____

_____

"My happiness is more important than being hurt and being bitter."

_____

_____

_____

_____

_____

_____

"I choose to uplift those who have hurt me, sending them positive energy and intentions."

_____

_____

_____

_____

"I forgive you. I am letting go of what happened between us and am moving on in my life."

_____

_____

_____

_____

_____

Today, I am happy and grateful for: *Date:* _____

_____

_____

_____

_____

"The past is over. I move beyond my mistakes and focus on living in the NOW."

_____

_____

_____

_____

_____

"I treat myself with respect and kindness from today forward."

_____

_____

_____

_____

_____

"I let go of all urges to criticize myself."

_____

_____

_____

_____

_____

_____

Today, I am happy and grateful for: Date: _____

_____
_____
_____
_____

"I am at peace with myself."

_____
_____
_____
_____
_____

"Who I am, exactly as I am, is truly beautiful."

_____
_____
_____
_____

"I am in charge of how I feel and today I'm choosing happiness."

_____
_____
_____
_____
_____

CREATING MIRACLES

Date: _____

_____

_____

_____

_____

"I am creating a beautiful life."

_____

_____

_____

_____

_____

"I choose to make the rest of my life
the best of my life."

_____

_____

_____

_____

_____

"I know I can create miracles in my life."

_____

_____

_____

_____

_____

_____

Today, I am happy and grateful for: Date: _____

_____
_____
_____
_____

"I open my heart to receive beautiful miracles and unlimited blessings."

_____
_____
_____
_____
_____
_____

"Every choice I make for myself is rooted in love."

_____
_____
_____
_____

"I am a magnet for positivity, abundance, and blessings."

_____
_____
_____
_____
_____

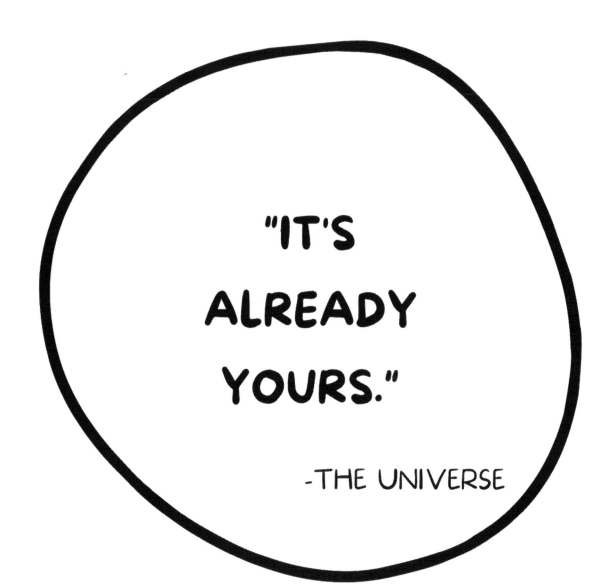

Today, I am happy and grateful for: *Date:* _____

_____
_____
_____
_____

"I deserve only good in my life."

_____
_____
_____
_____
_____

"I am capable of loving all of who I am."

_____
_____
_____
_____
_____

"I am at peace with myself."

_____
_____
_____
_____
_____

DESERVING OF TRUE LOVE

Today, I am happy and grateful for:　　Date: _____

_____
_____
_____
_____

"I deserve real and authentic love."

_____
_____
_____
_____
_____

"The love I seek is seeking me."

_____
_____
_____
_____
_____

"I am whole and completely ready for my life long partner."

_____
_____
_____
_____
_____

Today, I am happy and grateful for: *Date:* _____

_____
_____
_____
_____

"By _____ , I am in a happy, profoundly fulfilling relationship."

_____
_____
_____
_____
_____
_____

"I deserve the person I am seeking."

_____
_____
_____
_____
_____

"Being in love is effortless and easy."

_____
_____
_____
_____
_____

Today, I am happy and grateful for: *Date:* _____

_____

_____

_____

_____

"The love I desire is perfect for me."

_____

_____

_____

_____

_____

"I am healing my love story."

_____

_____

_____

_____

_____

"I am happy and grateful for the love in my life."

_____

_____

_____

_____

_____

Today, I am happy and grateful for: *Date:* _____

_____

_____

_____

_____

"I am an amazing catch."

_____

_____

_____

_____

_____

"I am successful in love."

_____

_____

_____

_____

"I am magnetic and irresistible to a positive, loving relationship."

_____

_____

_____

_____

_____

Today, I am happy and grateful for: *Date:* _____

_____

_____

_____

_____

"True love is available to me,
and I'm ready to receive it."

_____

_____

_____

_____

_____

_____

"I am aligned with the highest frequency of love."

_____

_____

_____

_____

_____

_____

"I am manifesting my dream love life."

_____

_____

_____

_____

_____

_____

Today, I am happy and grateful for: *Date:* _____

_____

_____

_____

_____

"I am loved beyond my wildest dreams."

_____

_____

_____

_____

_____

"I am stepping into the most loving decade of my life."

_____

_____

_____

_____

"The love I attract is better than I could have possibly imagined."

_____

_____

_____

_____

_____

Today, I am happy and grateful for: *Date:* _____

_____

_____

_____

_____

"From this moment on, I am attracting my soulmate."

_____

_____

_____

_____

_____

_____

"I feel the presence of my soulmate."

_____

_____

_____

_____

_____

"I am ready for miracles in my love life."

_____

_____

_____

_____

_____

DAY 58 ALIGNMENT WITH THE UNIVERSE

Today, I am happy and grateful for: *Date:* _____

_____
_____
_____
_____

"I am in alignment with my soulmate."

_____
_____
_____
_____
_____

"The Universe is bringing my soulmate to me now."

_____
_____
_____
_____
_____

"I visualize my soulmate so I can see them in my reality."

_____
_____
_____
_____
_____

GRATEFUL FOR MY SOULMATE

Today, I am happy and grateful for: Date: _____

_____

_____

_____

_____

"I am ready to meet the love of my life."

_____

_____

_____

_____

_____

"I love waking up with the love of my life. "

_____

_____

_____

_____

_____

"I am so grateful for my soul mate."

_____

_____

_____

_____

_____

MAKE A VISION BOARD

You've done such an amazing job throughout this journal! Take a minute to pat yourself on the back and be proud of yourself! You opened up your heart, identified, acknowledged and started the process of letting go of the guilt, regrets, and years of conditioning that were keeping you away from finding true love. You go girl! There's nothing stopping you now!

Through the process of journaling, visualizations played an important role in taking you forward to feeling the presence of true love in your life. In this section, you will take the visualizations one step forward and create a real, physical vision board!

Below, and in the next few pages, you will find vision board elements- graphics and quotes that summarize your journey throughout this journal. Cut-out the elements that resonate with you and along with the physical image you created on page ___, make a vision board to keep you reminded of your worth and readiness for true love.

You may use an opened-out delivery box, a small cork board or even a cereal box to paste these elements on and create the vision for your epic love story. Here's to getting another step closer to meeting the amazing man you're destined to be with!

I support my

deepest healing

SOULMATE TIMES

LATEST PREDICTION

My true love is going to find me, this year!

"THE UNIVERSE IS BRINGING MY SOULMATE TO ME NOW."

I feel the presence of my soulmate

I Deserve ALL the GReAT THINGS THAT I DReaM abOUT

SELF CARE IS NOT SELFISH

THE LOVE I ATTRACT IS BETTER THAN I COULD HAVE POSSIBLY IMAGINED

I AM READY FOR *miracles* IN LOVE

dear me,
YOU ARE READY FOR TRUE LOVE

I DESERVE THE LOVE I DESIRE.

I release all that no longer serves my higher good.

"I AM READY TO RECEIVE AN ABUNDANCE OF LOVE."

"The love I seek is seeking me."

"I trust. I believe. I receive."

Who I am, exactly as I am, is truly beautiful.

I know I can create miracles in my life.

I AM A MAGNET FOR ABUNDANCE AND LOVE.

Printed in Great Britain
by Amazon

45810864R00061